The Legend of Robin Hood

adapted from the classic adventure tale

book and lyrics by P. Haines-Ainsworth
music by Terence Alaric Levitt

published by winking kat books
winkingkatbooks.com

ROBIN HOOD
a musical adaptation in two acts

AUTHOR'S NOTES

This adaptation of the classic legend, **ROBIN HOOD**, was written with a great deal of silliness and humor. It features the main characters from the story, yet has a decidedly modern take. We've tried to retain some of the swashbuckling while reducing the actual violence and swordplay.

The play has several leading roles available for either male or female actors with many supporting roles. The ensemble can be reduced or increased based casting as written (49 roles) or doubling roles within the ensemble - particularly the poetry contestants, judges, and Marion's attendants. The roles of King Richard and Concord can also be doubled from the ensemble.

P. Haines-Ainsworth

"Robin Hood" was initially adapted for Emily Dickinson Elementary's Little Theater program in 2012. It was subsequently produced by other schools and by Tullahoma's Performing Arts for Children and Teens program in 2015.

CHARACTERS

Robin Hood (girl or boy)
Alan a'Dale (minstrel)
Will Scarlett
Little John
Friar Tuck (brews root beer)
Friar Philip
Forest elves (Laurel & Holly)
Merry Men (Michael, Slone, Parker)
Royal Herald

Sheriff of Nottingham
Sheriff's Nephew, Clyde (looses poetry contest with Robin)
Sheriff's deputies (2 deputies) Frank, Scott
Tax collector, Mr. de Plume
Prince John
Prince John's Counselor, Budge
King Richard
King Richard's messenger, Concord

Maid Marian
Marion's nurse (Bridgit)
Marion's attendants (Alison, Ardis, Astrid)
Randall, a poetry contestant
Poetry contestants (second round) Alvin, Margaret
Poetry Judges (3)
Villagers:

Beth	Katherine
Albert	Darby
Jenny	Charles
Keith	Lilly
Penelope	Tess
Jack	Nancy
Pheobe	Opal
Daisy	Rose

MUSIC CUE 1 – OVERTURE - ENTRANCE OF LAUREL & HOLLY

ACT ONE: SCENE 1
THE EDGE OF SHERWOOD FOREST

(forest elves, Laurel and Holly enter)

LAUREL
Good evening. Welcome to Sherwood Forest.

HOLLY
Sherwood Forest has been our home since before you were all born.

LAUREL
Since before the Beatles and Queen Elizabeth.

HOLLY
The first Queen Elizabeth.

LAUREL
I know we don't look very old, but we elves have lived in Sherwood Forest since the days of kings and legends.

HOLLY
Many famous and infamous people have also called this forest their home.

LAUREL
One of the most famous was the bandit, Robin Hood.

HOLLY
A bandit with a heart of gold.

LAUREL
He was a criminal.

HOLLY
Not really.

LAUREL
He took other people's money.

HOLLY
He only took money from bad and greedy people.

LAUREL
See. You agree that he stole other people's money.

HOLLY
Yes, but he didn't keep it. He (She) gave it away to help people who were poor and starving. The same people who had their money taken by the bad people in the first place.

LAUREL
This whole story is always so confusing.

HOLLY
Yes, it is. That's why we should simply act it out.

LAUREL
An excellent idea.

HOLLY
The tale of Robin Hood begins many, many years ago.

LAUREL
Hundreds.

HOLLY
A thousand almost.

LAUREL
Then, the great King Richard, the Lionheart, ruled the land of the Britons.

> *(Elves exit.)*

MUSIC CUE 2 – LAUREL AND HOLLY PLAYOFF

ACT ONE: SCENE 2
NOTTINGHAM SQUARE

> *(King Richard enters with Prince John and his group. Towns-people and Maid Marion and her group also enter)*

KING RICHARD
Good Subjects of Great Britain. I have an announcement to make. Some of my fellow kings and princes have gone to the Holy Land to fight. They have sent word to me that they need my help. So, I've decided to journey to the Holy Land to join them in battle.

TOWNSPEOPLE AND MARION'S GROUP
Hooray!!

KING RICHARD
While I'm gone, my brother, Prince John, will be in charge!

(Prince John steps forward to wave)

TOWNSPEOPLE AND MARION'S GROUP
(disappointedly)
Awwwww!

KING RICHARD
No. Really. Everything will be fine. I'll get to the Holy Land in a few months, help everyone win their battles, and before you know it, I'll be back here.

TOWNSPEOPLE
Hooray!!!

KING RICHARD
Now, wish me luck and say good-bye.

MUSIC CUE 3 - "FAREWELL TO KING RICHARD"

TOWNSPEOPLE AND MARION'S GROUP
> *GOOD-BYE TO YOU, KING RICHARD,*
> *THE BEST KING IN THE LAND.*
> *YOU LEAVE TODAY FOR FAR AWAY*
> *TO GIVE YOUR FRIENDS A HAND.*
>
> *BRAVE, BRAVE, KING RICHARD*
> *YOU'RE LOYAL AND TRUE BLUE.*
> *THOUGH YOU'LL BE GONE, LIFE WILL GO ON,*
> *BUT WE WILL ALL MISS YOU.*

(Musical interlude- Dance Break - 6 measures)

> *FAREWELL TO YOU, KING RICHARD.*
> *DO YOU REALLY HAVE TO GO?*
> *WERE THERE A WAY, WE KNOW YOU'D STAY.*
> *YOU HATE TO CAUSE US WOE.*
>
> *BRAVE, BRAVE, KING RICHARD*
> *YOU'RE LOYAL AND TRUE BLUE.*
> *WHILE YOU ARE GONE, WE HAVE PRINCE JOHN ...*

(spoken)
Uggh

WE GUESS HE'LL HAVE TO DO.
KING RICHARD, COME BACK SOON.

KING RICHARD
> *ADIEU!*

(Everyone exits except Prince John, Budge, Sheriff, and Clyde)

PRINCE JOHN
What do you think, Budge? You're my Counselor. What should I think about the crowd's reaction?

BUDGE
Your Majesty, I wouldn't take their reaction personally. I'm sure they didn't mean to be mean.

PRINCE JOHN
Yes, they did. Let's all be honest. The people hate me.

BUDGE
Hate is such a strong word, sire.

PRINCE JOHN
They like my brother, Richard, better.

SHERIFF
They just don't know you as well as we do, sire.

PRINCE JOHN
You know me best of all, Sheriff. Why don't the people like me?

SHERIFF
Probably because you are greedy, selfish, and bad-tempered.

PRINCE JOHN
Really?

SHERIFF
Yes. And that is why I DO like you.

PRINCE JOHN
Sheriff, we are two of a kind.

MUSIC CUE 4 – "TWO OF A KIND"

SHERIFF & PRINCE JOHN
(singing)
TWO OF A KIND
TWO BIRDS OF A FEATHER
WE'RE TWO OF A KIND
IN FAIR AND 'FOWL' WEATHER
IT'S ALWAYS THE SAME
THROUGH EVERY ENDEAVOUR
WE'RE EQUALLY BAD, EACH ONE A CAD, GENUINELY NASTY

SIMILAR MINDS
SO CUNNING AND CLEVER
FOREVER ALIGNED
THE YEARS CANNOT SEVER
THE STRONG TIES THAT BIND
WE TWO FRIENDS TOGETHER

PRINCE JOHN
EACH VILE DEED

SHERIFF
WE'RE SUCH BAD SEEDS

BOTH
PRETENTIOUSLY BOMBASTY.

PRINCE JOHN
SO WHEN HE GETS INTO A JAM
I'LL NEVER TURN AWAY

SHERIFF
'CAUSE IF I DO, I KNOW HE'LL SCRAM
AND LEAVE ME THERE TO PAY.

BOTH
I'M CERTAIN THAT IT'S TRUE BECAUSE
IT'S JUST THE THING THAT I WOULD DO…
AND WE ARE…

TWO OF A KIND
TWO BIRDS OF A FEATHER
WE'RE TWO OF A KIND

9

BOTH (continue)

> *IN FAIR AND FOWL WEATHER*
> *IT'S ALWAYS THE SAME*
> *THROUGH EVERY ENDEAVOUR*
> *LIKE MY REFLECTION, SHEER PERFECTION,*
>
> *YOU MAY THINK HE'D NEVER LET ME FALL.*
> *BUT SINCE WE'RE TWO OF A KIND*
> *I KNOW I CAN'T TRUST HIM… AT ALL.*

PRINCE JOHN
> *NOT AT ALL.*

SHERIFF
> *NOT AT ALL.*

PRINCE JOHN
(spoken)
Would you buy a used car from this man?

> *(end of song)*

PRINCE JOHN
I must admit, even though they don't like me, I have to keep the people happy or they might turn against me and rebel. There are a lot more of them than there are of us.

SHERIFF
Perhaps you could hold some kind of celebration or festival to entertain and distract them.

PRINCE JOHN
That's a good idea. Why didn't you think of that, Budge? You're supposed to be my counselor.

BUDGE
Well, I …

SHERIFF
We could have a contest. The people always love a chance to cheer for their favorite contestant.

BUDGE
And you can offer a prize to the winner. A large bag of gold coins!

PRINCE JOHN
A small one.

BUDGE
Yes, Sire. A small bag.

PRINCE JOHN
That's better. But what kind of contest?

BUDGE
What about an archery competition?

PRINCE JOHN
I don't think putting me in an arena with a bunch of angry citizens carrying bows and arrows is a particularly good idea – do you?

BUDGE
No, Sire.

SHERIFF
If I may make a suggestion, Highness. What about a poetry contest?

PRINCE JOHN
That sounds a lot safer. Why didn't you think of that, Budge?

BUDGE
Well, I…

PRINCE JOHN
We'll go with the poetry contest, and we'll hold it in Nottingham, if that's all right with you, Sheriff?

SHERIFF
My city would be honored, Sire.

PRINCE JOHN
Send in the Royal Herald.

SHERIFF
Send in the Royal Herald!

BUDGE
Send in the Royal Herald!

(herald enters)

PRINCE JOHN
(to herald)
I want you to travel to all corners of the kingdom and announce to the people that I, Prince John, will host a contest to see who is the best poet in the land. The contest will be held a week from today in Nottingham. The winner will receive a bag of gold coins – a small one.

HERALD
Very good, Sire. I will leave immediately.

> *(herald exits)*

PRINCE JOHN
There it is. Budge, come with me. I'll need your advice on what I should wear to the contest next week.

BUDGE
Yes, Sire.

> *(Budge and Prince John exit)*

CLYDE
The contest sounds like a lot of fun, uncle. I like poetry. I think I will enter.

SHERIFF
You will enter, Clyde. And you will win.

CLYDE
I will?

SHERIFF
Yes. I will make sure of it. We can't let any of the peasants get their hands on that gold. They wouldn't know what to do with it.

CLYDE
No, they wouldn't.

SHERIFF
I just have to bribe one of the judges with a small part of that gold. It should be easy. Go on, Clyde. Start working on your poem. It must at least be good enough to seem like it could win.

> *(Sheriff and Clyde exit)*

MUSIC CUE 5 - TRANSITION 1
ACT ONE: SCENE 3
SHERWOOD FOREST

(Friar Tuck and Friar Philip enter pulling a cart of barrels. Laurel and Holly peek out from behind a bush, giggle and run offstage)

FRIAR TUCK
Did you see that?

FRIAR PHILIP
See what? I did not see anything.

FRIAR TUCK
I think this forest is haunted.

FRIAR PHILIP
The only creatures that haunt Sherwood Forest are bandits. We need to hurry and get out of this forest before they steal our valuable cargo.

(enter Will Scarlet and the Merry Men, Michael, Slone, Parker, Little John, and Alan a'Dale)

WILL SCARLET
Did you say valuable cargo?

SLONE
I wonder what kind of cargo that might be.

PARKER
It must be valuable.

MICHAEL
Maybe it's gold or silver.

ALAN a'DALE
Maybe it's silk or fur.

FRIAR TUCK
We are only poor friars. We aren't allowed to have anything like that.

FRIAR PHILIP
It's not that valuable.

WILL
Let us decide. Tell us, Friar. What's in your wagon?

FRIAR TUCK
Root beer.

FRIAR PHILIP
Barrels and barrels of root beer.

PARKER
That's it? Just root beer?

SLONE
Root beer isn't worth anything.

FRIAR TUCK
Not worth anything? Root beer is the most amazing beverage in the world.

MUSIC CUE 6 -"THE ROOT BEER SONG"

FRIAR TUCK
Delicious

FRIAR PHILIP
Delectable

FRIAR TUCK
Delightful

FRIARS
Root Beer

> *(singing)*
> *WHEN YOU'RE THIRSTY. REALLY, REALLY THIRSTY.*
> *AND YOUR THROAT IS PARCHED AND DRY.*
> *AND THERE'S NOTHING, SIMPLY NOTHING,*
> *THAT CAN SEEM TO SATISFY.*
>
> *WE'VE THE ANSWER TO YOUR DRINKING PROBLEM.*
> *AS YOU SEE, WE CANNOT LIE.*
> *OUR TASTY TANGY, TRULY TEMPTING, ROOT-ER-IFFIC ROOT BEER*
> *IS THE BEST ROOT BEER YOU'LL EVER WANT TO TRY.*
> *(repeat melody)*

(Tuck) *JUST ONE MUG-FULL*
(Philip) *OR ONE JUG-FULL*

14

(BOTH) Root Beer!

MERRY MEN
> *WE HAVE SAMPLED FRIARS' ROOT BEER*
> *AND WE'RE HERE TO TESTIFY.*
> *THAT THE ROOT BEER HERE INSIDE THESE BARRELS*
> *IS THE BEST THAT YOU CAN BUY.*
> *THEIR TASTY TANGY, TRULY TEMPTING, ROOT-ER-IFFIC ROOT*
> *BEER IS THE BEST ROOT BEER YOU'LL EVER WANT TO TRY.*

FRIARS
> *FOAMY. SPARKLEY. SARSAPARILLA. SILKY. SPICY. SWEET BUR GOO.*

ALL
> *LICORICE, GINGER, AND VANILLA. BRIGHT, REFRESHING, BUBBLY*
> *   BREW.*
> *WHEN YOU'RE THIRSTY. REALLY, REALLY THIRSTY.*
> *AND YOUR THROAT IS PARCHED AND DRY.*
> *AND THERE'S NOTHING, SIMPLY NOTHING,*
> *THAT CAN SEEM TO SATISFY.*
> *TRY SOME ROOT BEER. TRY SOME FRIARS' ROOT BEER*
> *JUST ONE SIP AND YOU'LL KNOW WHY.*

FRIARS
> *OUR TASTY, TANGY, TRULY TEMPTING, ROOT-ER-IFFIC ROOT BEER*
> *IS THE BEST ROOT BEER YOU'LL EVER WANT TO BUY.*

ALL
> *THEIR TASTY TANGY, TRULY TEMPTING, ROOT-ER-IFFIC ROOT BEER*
> *IS THE BEST*

(Friar Tuck)   *ROOT BEER*
> *(Friar Philip)*   *ROOT BEER,*
>   *(Merry Men)*   *ROOT BEER…*

ALL
> *YOU'LL EVER WANT TO BUY.*

WILL SCARLET
Where were you going with your wagon of root beer?

FRIAR TUCK
To Nottingham.

FRIAR PHILIP
We were going to sell it at the poetry contest.

ALAN a'DALE
Poetry contest. That sounds like the perfect contest for a bard like me. It's about time they had a contest to test a man's brains instead of his muscles.

MICHAEL
You better not sing any of the songs you sing around here.

SLONE
That's right. No one would be able to hear the other contestants when all the dogs in Nottingham begin to howl.

WILL SCARLET
When is this contest to be held?

FRIAR TUCK
The day after tomorrow.

WILL SCARLET
Excellent! Gentlemen, what say you we give an escort to these two friars to make sure their root beer gets safely to Nottingham?

ALL MERRY MEN
Aye! That's a great idea!

WILL SCARLET
(to Friars)
It is decided, gentlemen. Let us go! On to Nottingham!

> (all exit except for Slone and Parker)

PARKER
I don't know about you, but I might get pretty thirsty on my way to Nottingham.

SLONE
Me, too.
> (Slone and Parker exit)

MUSIC CUE 7 – "ROOT BEER" PLAYOFF

ACT ONE: SCENE 4
       NOTTINGHAM SQUARE
There are flags and banners hanging in the square. There is a table with three chairs upstage on one side and a throne on the other.

(The Sheriff enters with Clyde. Frank and Scott enter from the opposite side)

SHERIFF
(to Frank and Scott)
Is everything arranged?

FRANK
Yes, sir. The head judge has given us his word that your nephew will win.

SHERIFF
How much did you pay him?

SCOTT
We didn't have to pay him anything. We told him if Clyde doesn't win, you'll put his whole family in jail.

SHERIFF
Even better. Go stand by the judges' table.

CLYDE
Here come the judges now.

(Judges walk in and take their seats at the table. The villagers enter including the Merry Men and the Friars. Herald enters)

HERALD
Ladies and Gentlemen, His Royal Highness, Prince John!

(Prince John enters waving. Everyone is quiet.)

ALBERT
(timidly)
Hooray!

VILLAGERS
(silent)

PRINCE JOHN
Tough crowd.

SHERIFF
Welcome, Your Highness.

PRINCE JOHN
I don't know, Sheriff. Are you really sure this was a good idea?

SHERIFF
Definitely, your Highness. Wait and see.

HERALD
Sheriff. Your Highness. I present the Lady Marian.

(Maid Marian enters with Bridgit and attendants.)

MAID MARIAN
Your Highness

(Maid Marian and her attendants courtesy in front of the Prince)

PRINCE JOHN
I have heard a lot about you, Lady Marian. You do not disappoint.

SHERIFF
Shall we begin, Sire?

PRINCE JOHN
Yes. Let's get this party started. *(to Marian)* I hope you will join me on the royal platform.

MAID MARIAN
Of course, Your Highness.

(Prince John and Budge cross to throne and Prince John sits. Marian and her attendants follow and stand around him)

SHERIFF
Herald! Call the first contestant.

HERALD
Will the first contestant for the poetry contest step forward.

(Randall steps center stage)

RANDALL
Your Highness, Ladies, and Gentlemen… and judges. My poem is called 'Sunlight'.
> Golden, glowing light
> Shining on the green meadow
> Makes me squint my eyes.
Thank you.

PRINCE JOHN
That was not a proper poem.

PENELOPE
It didn't even rhyme.

RANDALL
It was Haiku.

(Judges hold up voting cards with one's or zeros)

RANDALL
But Haiku is a legitimate form of poetry.

PRINCE JOHN
Not in England, sir! Next!

HERALD
Next!

(Randall exits. Alan a'Dale stands up and takes center stage. He clears his throat and signals pianist to strike chord. Piano underscores the next part of the monologue)

MUSIC CUE 8 – POEM UNDERSCORE with arpeggio

ALAN a'DALE
Ladies and Gentlemen,
Great to be back again,
Here in old Nottingham town.

If I may be so bold
My tunes are solid gold
Just like Prince John's shiny new crown.

(singing) SO......

JUDGE ONE
Wait one minute!

(Music stops suddenly)

JUDGE THREE
Are you going to sing?

ALAN a'DALE
Of course. I'm a balladeer. I always sing my poems.

JUDGE TWO
That is against the rules.

JUDGE THREE
This is a poetry contest, not a singing contest.

ALAN a'DALE
But I can't just speak my poems. They are meant to be sung to music.

JUDGE ONE
Then, sir, you are disqualified!

> *(Alan a'Dale exits. Clyde stands up and takes center stage. He clears his throat)*

CLYDE
> Roses are red.
> Violets are blue.
> I'm going to win the contest today,
> 'Cause I'm the sheriff's nephew.

> *(The Crowd applauds and Judges 1 & 2 hold up cards making the number 10. Judge 3 holds up the '0' card until the other judges remind him to hold up the '1' as well to make it read '10')*

> *(Robin steps forward)*

ROBIN
I can't believe you're giving his poem a '10'. That has to be the worst poem I've ever heard.

CLYDE
What do you know?

ROBIN
I know that part of your poem is as old as Sherwood Forest and the rest of it is just plain terrible. A poem should have rhythm and meter.

MUSIC CUE 9 – "ROBIN'S RAP"

> *(starts to speak in Rap. Crowd begins to clap along)*

ROBIN
> *YOU CALL YOURSELF A POET, BUT YOU DON'T REALLY KNOW*
> *IF YOU WANNA BE A POET THEN THE WORDS GOTTA FLOW.*
> *YOU CAN'T JUST PUT TOGETHER*
> *JUMPIN' JUMBLES OF LETTERS,*
> *YOU MUST SAY MORE THAN BLETHER*
> *TO DESERVE ALL THAT DOUGH.*

ROBIN (continues)
>*TO WIN THIS COMPETITION, MAN, YOUR POEM SHOULD HAVE*
>>*SOUL!*
>
>*AND MAKE THE PEOPLE STOMP THEIR FEET LIKE OLD ROCK 'N'*
>>*ROLL.*
>
>*YOU GOTTA GIVE YOUR POEM METER -- NEVER BE TERSE.*
>*YOU CANNOT BE A CHEATER,*
>*'LESS YOU'RE DOING BLANK VERSE.*

JUDGES
>*BLA…BLA, BLA, BLA…BLA.. BLANK VERSE.*
>
>*(everyone stops clapping)*

ROBIN
But no one really understands THAT kind of poem.
>*(back in rhythm)*
>*WHAT I'M SAYIN'S YOU'RE NO POET.*
>*YOU'RE JUST A PRETENDER.*
>*AND, SINCE ALL THE REST HAVE FALTERED,*
>*I'M THE LONE CONTENDER.*
>*SO, FIN'LY THE CONCLUSION OF THIS CONTEST MUST BE*
>*THAT UNDENIABLY, UNDOUBTEDLY, THE WINNER…*
>>*IS… ME!*

VILLAGERS
(cheer)

>*(Judges pick up bag of gold and start to present it to Robin.*
>*The Sheriff interrupts)*

SHERIFF
Wait a minute! You just said singing was illegal in this contest.

JUDGE ONE
But that wasn't singing.

JUDGE TWO
There was no melody. You can't call it singing when there is no melody, can you?

JUDGE THREE
(Shrugs as if to say 'I don't know')

ROBIN
Then, the prize belongs to me.

(Robin takes the bag of gold and runs off-stage)

CLYDE
But I got a perfect score!

SHERIFF
(to Clyde and his men)
After him! He can't go far carrying that heavy, little bag of gold.
Move out and capture him. Bring him back here!

> *(Sheriff, Clyde, and Sheriff's men chase after Robin. Townspeople leave. Prince John, Budge, Maid Marian, Bridgit and attendants move center stage)*

PRINCE JOHN
Well, that certainly did not turn out like I thought it would.

MAID MARIAN
No. It was much more exciting than I ever thought it would be.
Thank you for a wonderful afternoon, Your Highness.

> *(Maid Marian bows and exits with all her attendants)*

PRINCE JOHN
I hope the Sheriff catches him and brings my gold back.

BUDGE
Yes, Sire.

> *(The Herald runs in breathless)*

HERALD
Sire! Sire! I have important news!

PRINCE JOHN
What news?

HERALD
I have good news and bad news.

PRINCE JOHN
Tell us quickly!

HERALD
Which news do you want first?

PRINCE JOHN
Budge, which do I want first?

BUDGE
The bad news, Sire.

PRINCE JOHN
(to Herald)
Give me the bad news first.

HERALD
The bad news is that your brother, King Richard, was taken captive by the King of France on his way home.

PRINCE JOHN
Whew! That's not very bad news. What is the good news?

HERALD
While he is captive, you can declare yourself king.

PRINCE JOHN
That is very good news. I'm glad I saved the good news for last.
(to Budge)
Well, Budge, if I am King, I'm going to make some changes around here. Let's get started shall we?

(Herald and Prince John exit)

BUDGE
Oh, dear. This act did not end well at all. I hope you will come back to see if everything works out in Act 2.

MUSIC CUE 10 – VARIATION ON LAUREL AND HOLLY THEME

(Laurel and Holly enter)

LAUREL & HOLLY
Of course they will. Now let's go and let them get their refreshments.

(Holly claps her hands and the House Lights come on.)

(Music accompanies the fairies' dance as they chase Budge offstage)

END ACT ONE

ACT TWO: SCENE 1
Nottingham Square
(Townspeople enter downtrodden and trudging)

MUSIC CUE 11 - "TAXES"

TOWNSPEOPLE
> *SAUSAGE, SOUP, SAUERKRAUT*
> *KING JOHN TAXES EVERYTHING WE EAT.*

(spoken) **Everything!**
> *WALKING. SLEEPING. BREATHING TAX.*
> *TAXES FOR THE SHOES UPON OUR FEET.*
> *WHETHER WE'RE ONE OR ONE HUNDRED.*
> *ALL OF US MUST PAY OUR DUES.*
> *WHETHER WE LIKE IT OR NOT, WE CAN'T REFUSE.*

MEN	**LADIES**
EVERY CENT.	*NIGHT AND DAY.*

ALL
> *ALL OF US HAVE GOT TO PAY*
> *'YOU KNOW WHO!'*
> *STREUDEL, COWS, AND CUCKOO CLOCKS.*
> *THEY TAX US IF WE GIVE OUR DOGS A BONE*

ALBERT
(spoken) **Ruff. Ruff.**

ALL
> *LIFE IS REALLY FEUDAL HERE.*
> *WE GET TAXED ON EVERYTHING WE OWN.*
> *KING RICHARD, WHY DID YOU LEAVE US?*
> *DIDN'T YOU KNOW WHAT HE'D DO?*
> *DIDN'T YOU KNOW ALL THE WOE THAT WOULD ENSUE?*
> *EVERY CENT. NIGHT AND DAY.*
> *ALL OF US HAVE GOT TO PAY*

PEASANTS (1)
> *EVERY CENT. NIGHT AND DAY. ALL OF US HAVE GOT TO PAY..*
> *EVERY CENT...*

	PEASANTS (2)
NIGHT AND DAY	*EVERY CENT*
ALL OF US HAVE GOT TO PAY	*ALL OF US HAVE GOT TO PAY*
	EVERY CENT
EVERY CENT	*HAVE TO PAY*

ALL PEASANTS
YOU KNOW WHO

ROSE
(spoken)
Talk about squeezing blood from a turnip.

ALL TOWNSPEOPLE
Ouch!

CHARLES
Doesn't Prince John realize we have no money left?

BETH
Don't let any of the Sheriff's men hear you calling him Prince John.

KATHERINE
He's King John now.

ALBERT
All I can say is that it will be a happy day when King Richard comes home. I heard they're using our taxes to pay the ransom to get the King of France to release him.

DARBY
King Richard was kidnapped?

LILLY
Yes. And if we're paying taxes to get him released, I guess I can spare another bushel of wheat or two.

KEITH
But not for much longer.

(Townspeople exit)

MUSIC CUE 12 – "SCENE CHANGE - TAXES UNDERSCORE"

ACT TWO: SCENE 2
Sherwood Forest

(Robin enters.)

ROBIN
It seems like I've been wandering in this wood forever.

(Laurel and Holly enter)

LAUREL
Not forever. Just a few days.

HOLLY
In elven time that's not very long at all.

ROBIN
Well, I live in human time. And wandering for a few days in human time makes a human very hungry.

HOLLY
You have a bag of gold. Why don't you just buy yourself some food?

ROBIN
Because if I go into the city to buy food, I'll be arrested.

LAUREL
Oh. That means you're an outlaw.

ROBIN
Yes. I guess so. A hungry one.

HOLLY
We can take you to where the rest of the outlaws live. They have extra food.

ROBIN
There are other outlaws in the forest?

LAUREL
Yes. Lots of them.

HOLLY
Come this way. We'll show you.

(The elves lead Robin off stage. They exit.)

ACT TWO: SCENE 3
   The Merry Men's Camp in Sherwood Forest

MUSIC CUE 13 - TRANSITION 2

(Scene opens on a different part of the forest. The Merry Men & Friars enter and gather on one side of a bridge. Robin and the fairies enter on the opposite side of the bridge)

ROBIN
Thank you. I would never have found their camp without you.

LAUREL AND HOLLY
They are very good at hiding.

(elves hide)

ROBIN
(Calling to the camp)
Hello! Do you mind if I join you?

WILL
Not at all, stranger. Just come across the bridge.

ROBIN
Thank you.

(As Robin begins to cross, Little John starts to cross from the opposite side blocking Robin's crossing.)

ROBIN
Excuse me.

LITTLE JOHN
I'm walking here.

ROBIN
I'm trying to get to the other side.

LITTLE JOHN
So am I.

ROBIN
If you just back up for a moment and let me by, then you could walk to the other side.

LITTLE JOHN
Maybe you should back up.

ROBIN
Can't we compromise here?

LITTLE JOHN
Nope.

ROBIN
Then I suppose we have to see who will make room first.

> *(Alan gives Little John a pole. Laurel and Holly give Robin a pole. There is a brief battle between Little John and Robin and Robin is knocked off the log. As Little John reaches down to help Robin up, Robin pulls Little John in the stream. All begin laughing and the two combatants shake hands and help each other up out of the stream.)*

WILL
Welcome, Stranger. No hard feelings. It is just a little game we play with new arrivals.

> *(Laurel and Holly exit)*

ROBIN
No hard feelings taken. My name is Robin of Loxley.

ALAN a'DALE
We can't call you that. It's too long and it makes you seem too fancy for this bunch of Merry Men. We'll just call you Robin Hood, in honor of the hood you wear.

ROBIN
Merry Men? I thought you were a bunch of thieves and bandits, no offence.

LITTLE JOHN
We are a bunch of bandits, no offense taken.

ROBIN
How can robbers and thieves be called Merry Men?

MICHAEL
There's no reason bandits have to be mean and nasty.

WILL
(spoken to meter)
They always say that pirates are 'jolly'.
Hence the 'Jolly Roger' on their flag
We resemble pirates in many ways
Especially because we love our swag.

LITTLE JOHN
We're like pirates without boats.

MICHAEL
Without peg legs or eye patches.

PARKER
Like pirates without parrots.

SLONE
Without masts and battened hatches

WILL
We're like pirates only… nicer.

MUSIC CUE 14 - "MERRY MEN"

MERRY MEN & FRIARS
JOLLY ROGER'S ONLY BLACK AND WHITE
WE'RE MORE COLORFUL IN GREEN.
MERRY MEN ARE NEITHER GOOD NOR BAD
WE'RE SOMEWHERE IN BETWEEN.

WE HAVE A SACRED CODE OF HONOR
AND WE SWEAR A SACRED OATH.
WE SING HEIGH-HO AND NONNY NONNER,
AND WE ALWAYS TELL THE TROTH.

SLONE
(spoken)
Troth?

MERRY MEN & FRIARS
LIKE THE PIRATES WE CAN ALL SAY 'ARRR"
AND WHEN WE WALK, WE WALK WITH SWAGGER,
BUT WE'LL NEVER SAIL THE SEVEN SEAS
OR FIGHT WITH SWORD AND DAGGER.

GROUP ONE
WE HAVE A CHEST

THAT'S FILLED WITH GOLD

BUT WE TRY NOT TO BE GREEDY.

GROUP TWO
WE HAVE A CHEST

THAT'S FILLED WITH GOLD

(spoken)
We're not greedy!

WILL
I KEEP A COIN

MERRY MEN & FRIARS
HE KEEPS A COIN

OR TWO FOR ME.

MERRY MEN *(except Will Scarlet)* **& FRIARS**
(spoken)
Or two for you?

ALL MERRY MEN & FRIARS
> *BUT ALL THE REST GO TO THE NEEDY.*
>
> *JOLLY ROGER'S ONLY BLACK AND WHITE*
> *WE'RE MORE COLORFUL IN GREEN.*
> *MERRY MEN ARE NEITHER GOOD NOR BAD*
> *WE'RE SOMEWHERE IN BETWEEN.*
> *WE'RE VERY, VERY, MERRY, MERRY MEN.*
>
> ***(END SONG)***

WILL
There is one thing, Robin. If you wish to join our band of thieves you have to take the gold you have and put it into the chest.

> *(Will opens the chest. Robin sees the gold inside.)*

ROBIN
Where did you get all that gold?

PARKER
We steal it from the corrupt officials in the town.

MICHAEL
And from Prince John's tax collectors.

ROBIN
But you have so much gold already. Why do you need mine?

> *(Maid Marian enters with Bridgit and attendants)*

MARIAN
Because we need all the gold we can get.

> *(Will, Robin, and Merry Men all bow)*

MARIAN
(to Robin)
I remember you from the poetry competition. You were wonderful.

ROBIN
Thank you.

MARIAN
You see. Prince John and the Sheriff have taken so much gold and food from the people of Nottingham that they have nothing left to help feed their families. The Merry Men of Sherwood steal some of it back, then I sneek it into the city and give it back to the people so they don't starve.

ROBIN
It sounds like what you're doing is very dangerous.

ALISON
It is dangerous.

ARDIS
If the Sheriff finds out…

ASTRID
Lady Marian will be arrested.

ROBIN
But you are a lady, Lady Marian. You shouldn't have to risk your safety for the people of Nottingham.

MARIAN
I don't have to. I want to. I can't stand by and watch them go hungry just to make the Sheriff and Prince John richer.

BRIDGIT
Power to the People!
(she is embarrassed by her own outburst)
Sorry, m'lady.

MARIAN
I always hated lying and Prince John is lying to the people. He says he's collecting more taxes to rescue King Richard, but he's really keeping all the money for himself. I had to do something.

BRIDGIT
Besides she likes taking risks.

MARIAN
I must admit, I do like living dangerously.

MUSIC CUE 15 – "NOTTINGHAM LADIES"

MARION
(singing intro)
>AS A LADY, YOU'RE EXPECTED
>TO BE DAINTY AND PROTECTED
>AND LIVE HIGH UP IN A TALL I-VO-RY TOWER.

BRIDGIT AND ATTENDANTS
>AN I-VO-RY TOWER.

MARIAN
>BUT WHAT PEOPLE KEEP IGNORING
>IS A LIFE LIKE THAT IS BORING
>AND A LADY NEEDS MUCH MORE TO MAKE HER FLOWER.
>IN NOTTINGHAM CITY
>THE GIRLS AREN'T JUST PRETTY
>WE'RE ALSO VERY CLEVER AND REALLY QUITE BRIGHT
>WE USE OUR RESOURCES
>TO FIGHT THE KING'S FORCES
>AND SIDE WITH THE PEOPLE AGAINST THE KING'S MIGHT.

BRIDGIT AND ATTENDANTS
>WE SIDE WITH THE PEOPLE AGAINST THE KING'S MIGHT.

MARIAN
>TO FIND SATISFACTION
>WE ALL MUST TAKE ACTION
>AND DO WHAT WE CAN TO MAKE THIS A FAIR FIGHT
>I MAY BE A LADY
>BUT PRINCE JOHN'S SO SHADY
>I CAN'T JUST SIT STILL AND BE PATIENT AND POLITE

BRIDGIT AND ATTENDANTS
>WE CAN'T JUST SIT STILL AND BE PATIENT AND POLITE.

ALL LADIES
>DING DONG DERRY DO DERRY DERRY DOWN DOWN
>WE'RE TAKING BACK THE TREASURE AND JOHN'S GOLDEN
>>CROWN.
>DING DONG DERRY DO DERRY DERRY DOWN DOWN
>WE'RE TAKING BACK THE TREASURE AND JOHN'S GOLDEN
>>CROWN.

ALL LADIES (continue)
DING DONG DERRY DERRY DOWN.

MARIAN
THE SHERIFF MAY WONDER
WHO'S TAKEN THEIR PLUNDER
FROM UNDER THEIR NOSES LIKE THIEVES IN THE NIGHT
NOT ONE PERSON GUESSES
BECAUSE OF OUR DRESSES
THAT WE ARE THE ONES DOING WRONG TO MAKE RIGHT

BRIDGIT AND ATTENDANTS
THAT WE ARE THE ONES DOING WRONG TO MAKE RIGHT

ALL LADIES
DING DONG DERRY DO DERRY DERRY DOWN DOWN
WE'RE TAKING BACK THE TREASURE AND JOHN'S GOLDEN
CROWN.

DING DONG DERRY DO DERRY DERRY DOWN DOWN
WE'RE TAKING BACK THE TREASURE AND JOHN'S GOLDEN
CROWN.
DING DONG DERRY DERRY DOWN.

MARIAN
The townspeople of Nottingham have sent some food for you.
(motioning to her attendants to open their baskets) Ladies.

ALISON
What little they have.

ARDIS
Prince John and the Sheriff have taken almost everything.

ASTRID
They've taken the shirts off their backs.

BRIDGIT
They've even taken candy from the babies.

WILL
Now, they've gone too far.

MARIAN
I think I have a plan to end their greed, but I'm going to need this
chest of gold and another one just as full.

ALAN a'DALE
But we've robbed just about every greedy noble and counting house in the county. How can we get more gold?

MARIAN
If you could find a way to get the gold from the city treasury, that would buy what I need to bring Prince John to his knees.

ROBIN
If you need the money, I think I know a way to get it for you.

MARIAN
Thank you. *(to attendants)* Ladies! Let's take this chest of gold and hide it in my castle.

LADIES
Yes, my lady.

> *(The attendants pick up the chest and carry it offstage)*

MARIAN
Farewell, and be safe.

> *(Marian exits)*

MERRY MEN & FRIARS
We will my lady.

ALAN a'DALE
So, what is your plan, poet?

ROBIN
Gather close and I'll tell you.

> *(The Merry Men form a huddle and discuss Robin's plan. The huddle breaks apart)*

WILL
That just might work.

ROBIN
Of course, it will work. Now, let's get started.

> *(Robin, the Friars, and the Merry Men exit)*

ACT TWO: SCENE 4
A Street in Nottingham

MUSIC CUE 16 – TRANSITION 3

(Jack enters and stands on stage. Penelope and Tess begin to cross stage. As they pass Jack, he calls them back)

JACK
Pssst.

PENELOPE
What is it?

TESS
You aren't going to try and tell us another joke are you?

PENELOPE
We're not in the mood for jokes today.

TESS
That's right. The tax collector is coming tomorrow.

JACK
I know. That's why I have some gold for you.

TESS & PENELOPE
Hooray!

JACK
Shhh! Not so loud. We don't want the Sheriff's men to hear.

(Jack starts passing out the gold to Tess and Penelope when Nancy comes running in.)

NANCY
Did you hear? Someone has robbed the city treasury!

TESS
(to Jack)
Is that where you got this gold?

JACK
No. I got this from Lady Marian's nurse, Bridgit.

NANCY
The word on the street is that the Merry Men of Sherwood Forest took the gold out of the treasury. They were led by the poet, Robin Hood.

PENELOPE
The Sheriff cannot be very happy today.

TESS
It's not a good idea to be on the streets when he's in a bad mood.

JACK
We should go home and act like nothing has happened.

TESS
And tomorrow we will pay our taxes with Prince John's own gold.

    (All exit)

MUSIC CUE 17 – TAXES TRANSITION

ACT TWO: SCENE 5
    King (Prince) John's Throne Room

    (King -aka Prince-John is sitting on his throne and talking with Budge. The Sheriff, Clyde, Frank, Scott, and Mr. de Plume enter)

SHERIFF
You're Highness.

PRINCE JOHN
Uh, uh, ahhhh! I'm king now, so you must call me, 'Your Majesty".

SHERIFF
Very well. Your Majesty. The treasury in Nottingham has been robbed.

PRINCE JOHN
Robbed?

SHERIFF
Robbed! They've taken everything!

PRINCE JOHN
How much was in the vault?

SHERIFF
Tax Collector! How much was in the treasury?

MR. D'PLUME
Two hundred and eighty thousand pounds, Sire. And fifteen pence.

PRINCE JOHN
This is an outrage! We need to arrest someone!

BUDGE
Who, Sire?

PRINCE JOHN
I don't know! But someone must be arrested!

SHERIFF
I believe it was the group of bandits who call themselves the Merry Men, your Majesty. And the leader of the group appears to be the varlet who won your poetry contest last month.

PRINCE JOHN
The poet who stole my bag of gold?

CLYDE
The very one, Sire.

PRINCE JOHN
We must arrest him! These Merry Men have gotten too bold. Robbing a carriage or two is one thing, but robbing the city treasury is another. That is my money! I cheated the people out of it fair and square!

SHERIFF
They say the Merry Men hide in Sherwood Forest. Clyde! Take your men to Sherwood Forest, find these villains, and bring them in.

CLYDE
But Uncle Giles, Sherwood Forest is a scary place.

FRANK
They say there are ghosts in there.

SCOTT
And nasty, zombie elves.

SHERIFF
I don't want to hear any excuses. GO!!!

(Clyde, Scott, & Frank exit)

BUDGE
Sherwood Forest is a big place. It may be difficult to find them there.

PRINCE JOHN
Not you, too, Budge.

BUDGE
I'm just saying. May I suggest something, Sire?

PRINCE JOHN
I am the King, Budge! If I want advice, I'll ask someone for it. *(pause)* What would you suggest?

BUDGE
This Robin Hood thinks he is the best poet in the land. If you had another poetry contest, I'm sure he could not resist entering to prove he is a better poet than anyone else.

PRINCE JOHN
Does this mean I will have to offer another bag of gold as a prize?

BUDGE
Probably a bigger one than last time to make sure he'll come.

PRINCE JOHN
But what if he takes this one, too.

SHERIFF
Don't worry, Your Majesty. My men will be ready this time. We'll arrest Robin Hood before his hand touches the bag.

PRINCE JOHN
I like the way you think, Sheriff.

SHERIFF
That's because we think alike.

MUSIC CUE 18 – "TWO OF A KIND" (reprise)

PRINCE JOHN & SHERIFF
> *TWO OF A KIND*
> *TWO BIRDS OF A FEATHER.*
> *WE'RE TWO EVIL MINDS*
> *THAT WORK WELL TOGETHER.*
> *IT'S ALWAYS THE SAME*
> *THROUGH EVERY ENDEAVOUR*

SHERIFF
> *LIKE MY REFLECTION*
> *SHEER PERFECTION,*

PRINCE JOHN
> *THROUGH IT ALL YOU'D NEVER LET ME FALL.*
> *BECAUSE WE'RE TWO,*

SHERIFF
> *BECAUSE WE'RE TWO,*

PRINCE JOHN & SHERIFF
> *BECAUSE WE'RE TWO, TWO OF A KIND.*

> *(Prince John, Sheriff, and Budge exit – taking throne with them)*

ACT TWO: SCENE 6
The Merry Men's Headquarters in Sherwood Forest

> *(Robin and the Merry Men are celebrating and counting the gold. Bridgit and Maid Marian's attendants enter.)*

BRIDGIT
Good day! This is very exciting. Lady Marian will be very happy.

ASTRID
Now, she can put her plan in place.

ALISON & ARDIS
And put an end to Prince John's tyranny!

ROBIN
Are they talking about us in the town?

BRIDGIT
Oh, yes. But that is old news. There is new news in town now.

ROBIN
What news?

BRIDGIT
Prince John has announced that he is having another poetry contest.

ASTRID
And this time he's offering a big bag of gold as a prize.

ROBIN
Another poetry contest?

WILL
It's obviously a trap to lure you into Nottingham and capture you.

ROBIN
I know you're right. The Sheriff must think we're not very smart, but I still want to enter the contest.

WILL
Ladies, take this chest of gold to Lady Marian so she can put her plan into place.

(Bridgit and the attendants exit carrying the gold.)

ROBIN
Merry Men, I think I have a plan to embarrass the Sheriff and get a big bag of gold in the bargain. To Nottingham!

(Robin and Merry Men exit)

MUSIC CUE 19 – TRANSITION - NOTTINGHAM LADIES
ACT TWO: SCENE 7
Nottingham Square

(Phoebe and Ian enter with the table for the judges)

PHOBE
The last time they had one certainly didn't go as planned.

IAN
Maybe that's why they're having another one.

(Daisy, Opal, and Rose enter carrying the chairs for the judges and place them behind the table.)

DAISY
I hope they have food this time.

OPAL
Me, too. I'm very hungry.

ROSE
Here come the judges.

> *(Judges enter and sit at the table. Charles, Beth, Katherine,
> Darby, Jenny, and Lilly enter followed by Astrid, Ardis,
> and Alison. The townspeople take their places to watch.)*

> *(Will, Alan, Little John, and the Merry Men enter in disguise and
> stand scattered about the crowd.)*

> *(The Herald enters.)*

HERALD
(announcing to the crowd)
People of Nottingham, His Majesty King John and His Honor, the
Sheriff of Nottingham.

> *(Prince John, the Sheriff, Clyde and Budge enter)*

CHARLES
(quickly)
Yay!

SHERIFF
Let's get this over with.

PRINCE JOHN
Wait a minute! Where is Lady Marian? I was hoping she'd be here.

ARDIS
(stepping forward)
Lady Marion could not make it today, your Majesty.

ALISON
She's has family visiting.

ASTRID
And she has a cold.

PRINCE JOHN
Too bad. Well, then, let's get on with it.
> *(to the crowd)*

Loyal Subjects! I, King John, proclaim this poetry contest open to the public. The winner will get this much larger bag of gold.

> *(Budge holds up a bag of gold.)*

PRINCE JOHN
So, if any of you have a poem, come forward and let us hear it.

> *(Robin steps out in disguised as an old man or woman)*

ROBIN
I have a poem.

SHERIFF
We're expecting a different contestant.

ROBIN
You said anyone could enter.

SHERIFF
Very well. Say your poem quickly.

ROBIN
Roses are red. Violets are blue.
Robin Hood made a fool out of you.

> *(Judges hold up their 10 point paddles.)*

CLYDE
You stole my poem!!

SHERIFF
That's not all he stole!

> *(The Sheriff removes Robin's disguise to reveal the real poet.)*

SHERIFF
That wasn't as good as your other poem, Robin Hood.

ROBIN
Maybe not, but I will still get the bag of gold.

SHERIFF
I wouldn't be too sure of that, if I were you. You see, I know some poetry myself.

"Roses are red
And Violets are blue."
The King and I
Were expecting you.

AH, Ha !!!

> *(Clyde, Budge, and the Sheriff surround Robin.)*

ROBIN
Your poem is good, but my poems are still better.
Sheriff, be nimble.
Sheriff, be quick.
We all knew this contest
Would be a trick.

Ah, HA !!!

> *(The Merry Men all pull back their hoods to show themselves.)*

SHERIFF
You think you're so smart, but I will have the last 'Ah Ha'.

Robin Hood be prepared for a fall
For my surprise has stumped you all.
I've brought all the king's horses and all the king's men.
To arrest Robin Hood and your merry, green friends.

> *(Frank, Scott, de Plume, and peasants doubling as guards enter and surround Robin and the Merry Men.)*

SHERIFF
AH. HA !!!
You are all under arrest.

PRINCE JOHN
Splendid! Good work, Sheriff! Now, by order of the King -- me, I command that Robin Hood and all the Merry Men be sent to the dungeons for life.

> *(King Richard enters with Lady Marian and Bridgit)*

KING RICHARD
By who's order, little brother?

PRINCE JOHN
Mine.

KING RICHARD
But now that I'm back, you're not King anymore, are you?

PRINCE JOHN
No.

KING RICHARD
So, you can't give orders like that, can you?

PRINCE JOHN
No.

KING RICHARD
But, I can. So, by the order of King Richard, I command that Robin Hood and all the Merry Men be pardoned of their crimes since they did them to help rescue me and for the welfare of the people of England.

JUDGE ONE
Hooray for King Richard

TOWNSPEOPLE AND MERRY MEN
(except Sheriff, Prince John, and Clyde)
Hip Hip Hooray! Hip Hip Hooray! Hip Hip Hooray!

KING RICHARD
(to Prince John)
Now, little brother, you and your friend better get on your hors-es and ride to Ireland or France or Spain or somewhere far away before I forget that you didn't use the gold you collected to pay my ransom so I could come home.

> *(Prince John, the Sheriff, and Clyde exit. Budge starts to leave, but Richard calls him back.)*

KING RICHARD
(to Budge)
You! Come back here. You are going to take that large bag of gold and give all the coins that my brother stole back to the citizens of Nottingham.

TOWNSPEOPLE, MERRY MEN, & LADIES
Hooray!

MUSIC CUE 20 – "FAREWELL, KING RICHARD" (reprise)

TOWNSPEOPLE
BRAVE, BRAVE, KING RICHARD
YOU'RE LOYAL AND TRUE BLUE.
WE HOPE TODAY, YOU'RE HERE TO STAY
BECAUSE WE ALL MISSED YOU.

(Dance Break)

BRAVE, BRAVE, KING RICHARD
PLEASE, SAY YOU'LL NEVER ROAM.
WE ALL ATTEST TO THIS REQUEST
WE NEED YOU HERE AT HOME.

KING RICHARD
Very well. I promise I'll stay.

TOWNSPEOPLE, MERRY MEN, & LADIES
Hooray!

(All exit except Marian, Bridgit, and Robin)

ROBIN
So, you used the gold to ransom King Richard.

MARIAN
Prince John wasn't going to do it, so someone had to.

ROBIN
You saved all of us from prison.

BRIDGIT
I think the least you could do would be buy her a root beer.

ROBIN
I will happily buy one for each of you.

(Robin, Marian, and Bridgit exit. Laurel and Holly enter)

LAUREL
And Sherwood Forest returned to being the quiet place it had been before Robin Hood and the Merry Men.

HOLLY
Quiet and peaceful. The perfect kind of place for elves, don't you think?

LAUREL AND HOLLY
We do! Good night.

MUSIC CUE 21 - BOWS

CURTAIN

SOUND AND MUSIC CUE LISTINGS

SUGGESTED PROP LIST

Small bag of gold
Larger bag of gold
Chest with gold
Barrels of Root Beer
Mugs for Root Beer
Cart
Number paddles for judges
Baskets
Trumpet for Herald (optional)
Scroll for Herald
Necklace of office for Sheriff'

vocal score

Farewell, King Richard

Pat Haines-Ainsworth

Terence Alaric

♩ = 116

Peasants

Piano

Good-bye to you, King

Rich- ard; the best king in the Land You leave to-day for

Copyright © 2012

50

far a way   to give your friends a hand.   Brave,   brave, King

Rich ard;   you're loy - al and true blue.   Though you'll be gone,   Life

will go on;   but we will all miss you.

DANCE

Fare - well to you, King Rich ard; do you real-ly have to

go? Were there a way, we know you'd stay; you hate to cause us

woe. Brave, brave, King Rich ard;, you're loy - al and true

blue. While you are gone, we have Prince John.. (ahh...) We

46
Peasants
guess he'll have to do.
King
Pno.
49
K. Rich:
Peasants
Rich ard... come back soon. A - dieu!
Pno.

Two of a Kind

Pat Haines-Ainsworth

Terence Alarie Levitt

Both
al-ways the same through ev-'ry en-dea - vor. We're e-qual-ly bad, each one a cad,
Pno.
Both
gen-u-ine-ly nas-ty.... Sim-i-lar minds so cun-ning and clev - er.... For
Pno.
Both
ev-er a - ligned: the years can-not sev - er.... the strong ties that bind we
Pno.
Both
two friends to - geth - er. Each vile... deed, we're such bad seeds; Pre-
John
Sheriff
Pno.

Both: ten-ti-ous-ly bom-bas-ty.___

John: So when he gets in-to a jam__ I'll

Sheriff: ne-ver turn a-way; 'cause if I do I know he'll scram and

Both: leave me here to pay. I'm cer-tain that it's true be-cause it's

Both: just the thing that I would do and we___ are___

Both

Two of a kind__ two birds of a feath - er.__ We're two of a kind__ in

Pno.

Both

fair and "fowl" weath - er.__ It's al-ways the same, through ev-'ry en-dea - vor.

Pno.

Both

Like my re - flec - tion, sheer per - fec - tion; You may

Pno.

Both

think he'd ne-ver let me fall. But since we're two of a kind, I

Pno.

know I can't trust him_____ at all,

not at all_____

not at all_____

Would you buy a used car from this man?

Root Beer Song

Pat Haines-Ainsworth

Terence Alaric Levitt

♩ = 120

De-li cious! De-lec-ta-ble! De-light ful!_ Root beer!

F. Tuck   F. Philip   F. Tuck   Friars

Piano

Friars

When you're thirs-ty, real ly, real-ly thirs-ty and your

Pno.

Friars

throat is parched and dry_ And there's noth-ing.

Pno.

Friars

simply noth-ing that can seem to sat - is - fy____

Pno.

Friars

We've the an-swer to____ your drink-ing pro-blem as you see, we can-not lie.

Pno.

Friars

Our tas-ty, tang-y, tru-ly tempt-ing, root-er - if - fic root beer is the

Pno.

61

Friars: best root beer you'll ev-er want to try.

F. Tuck / **F. Philip** / **Friars:** Just one mug full, or one jug full, and you'll kiss your thirst good bye.

Merry Men: We have sam-pled Fri-ar's root beer and we're

Root Beer
Merry Men
here to tes - ti - fy
That the root beer here
Pno.
Merry Men
Friars
in-side these bar-rels is the best that you can buy
Our
Pno.
Friars
tas-ty, tang-y, tru-ly tempt-ing, root-er - if - fic root beer is the best root beer you'll
Pno.

Friars
ev-er want to try.
All
Foam-y, spar-kley, sars-'pa-ril-la, silk-y, spi-cy, sweet bar-goo;
Pno.
All
Lic-'rice, gin-ger, and van-il-la, bright, re-fresh-ing bub-bly brew.
Pno.
All
When you're thirs-ty, real-ly, real-ly thirs-ty and your throat is parched and dry.
Pno.

All
Pno.
And there's noth - ing, sim - ply noth - ing that can
seem to sat - is - fy
Try some root beer, try
some Fri - ar's Root Beer just one sip and you'll know why
(Friars)
Our

59
Bbm A°/C Bbm/Db A°/C Bbm A°/C Db Bb°/D Db/Eb
Friars
tas-ty, tang-y, tru-ly tempt-ing, root-er-if-fic root beer is the best root beer you'll
Pno.
62
Eb7 Ab
All
Bbm A°/C Bbm/Db A°/C Bbm A°/C Db Bb°/D
Friars
ev-er want to buy. Their tas-ty, tang-y, tru-ly tempt-ing, root-er-if-fic root beer is the
Pno.
(F. Tuck)
best root beer,
Merry Men
best root beer
All
65
A.
Best root beer
you'll ev-er want to buy.
(F. Phiip)
Pno.

Robin's Rap

Pat Haines-Ainsworth

Terence ALaric Levitt

You call your-self a po-et but you

10
Robin
don't real-ly know; if you wan-na be a po-et then the words got ta flow... You
Pno.
13
Robin
can't just put to - geth - er jump - in' jum - bles of let - ters, you
Pno.
15
Robin
must say more than ble - ther to de - serve all that dough...
Pno.

18
Robin
Pno.
To
21
Robin
win this com - pe - ti - tion. Man, your po - em should have soul, and
Pno.
23
Robin
make the peo - ple stomp their feet like old rock 'n' roll
You
Pno.

Robin: got ta give your po-em me-ter, ne-ver be terse,... you can-not be a cheat-er 'less you're

Robin: do-ing blank verse.___

Judges: Bla-bla - bla - bla - bla blank verse.

Robin: ("But no one really understands that kind of poem.")

Robin: What I'm say-in's you're no po - et you're just a pre - ten - der

Robin: And since all the rest have fal-tered I'm the lone con - ten - der.... So,

Robin: fin - 'ly the con - clu-sion of this con-test must be that un - de

Robin: ni - a - bly, un-doubt-ed - ly the win-ner is me!

Taxes

Pat Haines-Ainsworth

Terence Alaric Levitt

72

15
Peasants
breath-ing tax.
Tax-es for the
Pno.
19
Peasants
shoes up-on our feet.
Whe-ther we're one or one hun-dred
Pno.
23
Peasants
All of us must pay our dues.
Whe-ther we like it or not, we can't re -
Pno.
27
Peasants
fuse.
Ev-er-y cent.
Pno.

Night and day... All of us have got to pay. You know who'...

Streu-del, cows, and cuc-koo clocks.

They tax us when we give our dog a bone. Ruff Ruff

Life is real- ly feu-dal here. We get

Taxes

Peasants: taxed on ev-'ry thing we own King Rich-ard, why... did you leave us? Did-n't you know what he'd do? Didn't you know all the woe that would en- sue? Ev-er-y cent. Night and day. All of us have got to pay.

66
Peasants
Ev-er-y cent. Night and day... All of us... have got to pay
Harmonious peasants
Ev - er-y cent. All of us... have got to pay
Pno.
70
Peasants
Ev-er-y cent... You know
Harmonious peasants
Ev-er-y cent. have to pay... You know
Pno.
74
Peasants
who! Ouch!
Harmonious peasants
who! Ouch!
Pno.

Merry Men (hornpipe)
(e minor)

Patricia Haines-Ainsworth

Terence Alarie

Jol - ly Ro - ger's on - ly black and white;

we're more co-lor-ful in Green _____ Mer-ry

Men are nei-ther good nor bad; we're some-where

in be-tween. We have a sa-cred code of

Merry Men
ho - nor and we swear a sa - cred oath
Pno.
29
Merry Men
We sing, "Hey ho" and "non - ny non - ner", and we al - ways tell the
Pno.
Kelly:
Solo lines
Troth?!
Merry Men
troth. Like the pi - rates we can all say.
Pno.

"Arrr!"; and when we walk, we walk with swag ger

But we'll ne - ver sail the sev - en seas, or

fight with sword and dag - ger

53
Merry Men group 1
We have a chest... that's filled with gold...
Merry Men group 2
We have a chest... that's filled with
Pno.

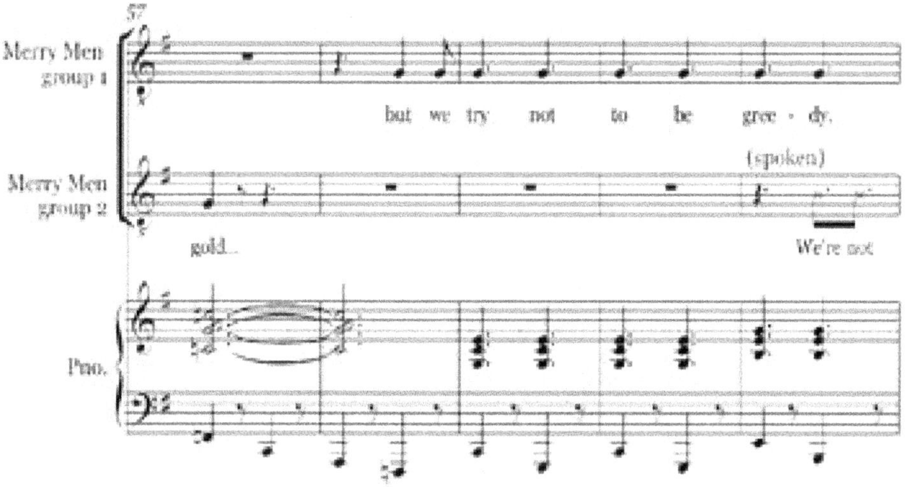
57
Merry Men group 1
but we try not to be gree - dy.
Merry Men group 2
(spoken)
gold... We're not
Pno.

62
Will Scarlett:
Solo lines
I keep a coin... or two for me.
Merry Men group 1
He keeps a coin...
Merry Men group 2
gree - dy! or two for
Pno.

67
All:
Solo lines
But all the rest goes to the need - y.
Merry Men group 1
But all the rest goes to the need - y.
Merry Men group 2
you? But all the rest goes to the need - y.
Pno.

Merry Men group 1: Jol - ly Ro - ger's on - ly black and

Merry Men group 2: Jol - ly Ro - ger's on - ly black and

Merry Men group 1: white; we're more co - lor-ful in Green

Merry Men group 2: white; we're more co - lor-ful in Green

83
Merry Men group 1
Mer - ry Men are nei - ther good nor bad; we're
Merry Men group 2
Mer - ry Men are nei - ther good nor bad; we're
Pno.
87
Merry Men group 1
some - where in be - tween. We're ver-y
Merry Men group 2
some - where in be - tween.
Pno.
92
Merry Men group 1
mer - ry, mer - ry
Merry Men group 2
ver - y mer - ry, mer - ry,
Pno.

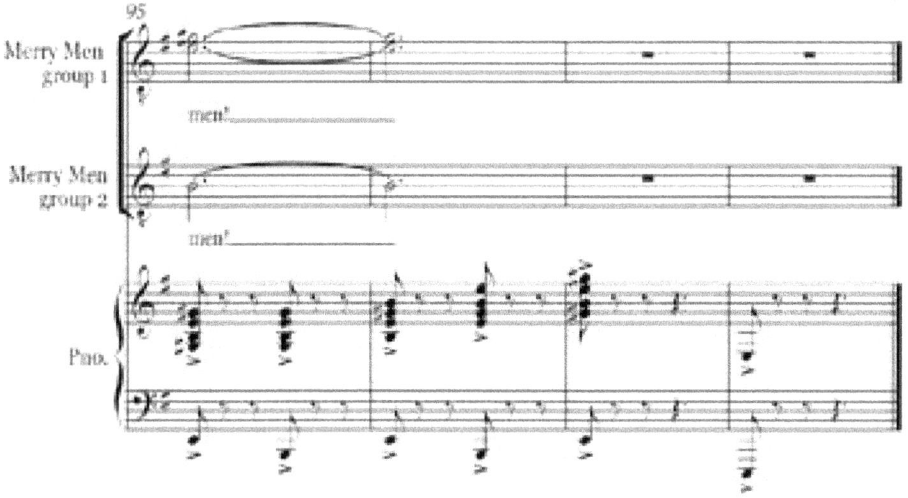
95
Merry Men
group 1
men!
Merry Men
group 2
men!
Pno.

8. The Nottingham Ladies

Pat Haines-Ainsworth

Terence Alaric

As a la-dy, you're ex-pect-ed to be dain-ty and pro-tec-ted and live high up in a tall i-vo-ry tow-er.

Bridgit and attendants:

An i-vo-ry tow-er.

But what peo-ple keep ig-nor-ing is a life like that is

86

Marian: bor-ing, and a la-dy needs much more to make her flow-er...

Marian: In Not-ting-ham Ci-ty the girls aren't just pret-ty. We're

Marian: al-so ver-y clev-er and real-ly quite bright. We use our re-sour-ces to

36
Marian
fight the king's for-ces and side with the peo-ple a - gainst the king's might.
all Ladies:
Ladies
We
Pno.
42
Marian
To find sat - is - fac-tion we
Ladies
side with the peo-ple a - gainst the king's might.
Pno.
48
Marian
all must take ac-tion and do what we can to make this a fair fight. I may be a
Pno.

4

Marian: la- dy, but Prince John's so shad-y, I can't just sit still and be pa- tient and po

Marian: lite.

Ladies: We can't just sit still and be pa-tient and po - lite.

Ladies: Ding dong der-ry do der - ry, der-ry down down, we're

68

Marian

Ding dong der-ry do der-

Ladies

tak-ing back the trea-sure and John's......gold-en cro-wown. Ding dong der-ry do der-

Pno.

71

Marian

- ry, der-ry down down; we're tak-ing back the trea-sure and John's......gold-en cro-wown.

Ladies

- ry, der-ry down down; we're tak-ing back the trea-sure and John's......gold-en cro-wown.

Pno.

6

Marian: The sher-iff may

Ladies: Ding, dong, der-ry, der-ry, down.

Marian: won-der who's tak-en their plun-der from un-der their nos-es like thieves in the

Marian: night. Not one per-son gues-ses be-cause of our dres-ses that we are the ones do-ing

Marian: wrong to make right.

Ladies: that we are the ones do-ing wrong to make right.

Ladies: Ding dong der - ry do der - ry, der - ry down down; we're

Marian: Ding dong der ry do der-

Ladies: tak-ing back the trea-sure and John's__ gold-en cro-wown. Ding dong der ry do der-

8

Marian: - ry, der-ry down down; we're tak-ing back the trea-sure and John's___gold-en cro - wown.

Ladies: - ry, der-ry down down; we're tak-ing back the trea-sure and John's___gold-en cro - wown.

Marian: Ding dong do, ding dong, der-ry, der-ry down. down.

Ladies: Ding dong do, der-ry, der-ry down. down.

9. Two of a Kind reprise

Pat Haines-Ainsworth

Terence Alaric Levitt

94

2 of a Kind reprise

Prince & Sheriff:
Like my re-flec-tion, sheer per-fec-tion; Through it
all you'd ne-ver let me fall. Be-cause we're
two, be-cause we're two, be-cause we're two, two of a kind.

King Richard reprise

Pat Haines-Ainsworth

Terence Alaric Levitt

Copyright © 2013

Lyrics: Brave, brave, King Rich ard, you're loy‑al and true blue. We hope to‑day you're here to stay be cause we all missed you.

King Richard reprise

Brave, brave, King Rich- ard,... please say you'll ne-ver roam. We all at-test to this re-quest, We

23
K. Rich:
Towns.
need you here at home. Ve-ry
Pno.
26
Peas.
Towns.
well, I pro-mise I'll stay. Hoo - ray!
Pno.

OTHER PLAYS AVAILABLE AT WINKING KAT BOOKS

NON-MUSICAL

Shakespeare 101

Who Stole the Queen of Hearts' Tarts?

Aesop's Fables

The Tiger, The Rabbit, and the Rescue of Spring

Yeh-Shen, a Chinese Cinderella story

Puss 'n Boots

MUSICAL (one or two acts)

The Day Zero Left Dodge; a mathematical Western

Treasure Island

Bayou Bug Tales (based on The Ant and the Grasshopper fable)

The Town Mouse and the Country Mouse

The Scarecrow (based on a short story by Washington Irving)

Arcani and The Dreaming Tree, based on a Bolivian folktale

The Barber's Wife, based on a trickster tale from India

The Dancing Princess, loosely based on a Ukranian fairy tale

Puss 'n Boots

Aesop's Fables

Yeh-Shen

For production rights contact:
    winkingkatbooks@gmail.com

        or write:
            Winking Kat Books
            17723 Tester Road
            Snohomish, WA 98290